STECK-VAUGHN

Level B

LANGUAGE
Exercises

TEACHER'S
GUIDE

Betty Jones
Saranna Moeller
Cynthia T. Strauch

STECK-VAUGHN
C O M P A N Y
ELEMENTARY • SECONDARY • ADULT • LIBRARY

Table of Contents

Acknowledgments

Executive Editor: Diane Sharpe
Supervising Editor: Stephanie Muller
Project Editor: Patricia Claney
Design Manager: Laura Cole
Illustrations: Holly Cooper and Gary Gattis

LANGUAGE EXERCISES Series:

Level A	Level D	Level G
Level B	Level E	Level H
Level C	Level F	Review

Language Exercises is a program designed for students who require additional practice in the basics of effective writing and speaking. Focused practice in key grammar, usage, mechanics, and composition areas helps students gain ownership of essential skills. The logical sequence of the practice exercises, combined with a clear and concise format, allows for easy and independent use.

Focus on Key Skills

Language Exercises provides systematic, focused attention to just one carefully selected skill at a time. Lessons are organized around a series of units. Level B provides a substantial Study Skills unit at the beginning of the book. This unit includes such skills as following directions, making comparisons, organizing information, alphabetical order, and using a dictionary. The remaining units are arranged in a logical sequence beginning with vocabulary, progressing through sentences, grammar and usage, mechanics, and culminating with composition skills.

Skills are reviewed thoroughly in a two-page Review at the conclusion of each unit and in the twelve-page Final Review at the end of the book. Also, the last twelve pages of this Teacher's Guide provide six two-page blackline master Unit Tests presented in a standardized test format. The content of each unit is repeated and expanded in subsequent levels as highlighted in the Scope and Sequence chart on the next two pages.

Application Is the Key

Throughout the program, *Language Exercises* stresses the application of language principles. In addition to matching, circling, or underlining elements in a predetermined sentence, lessons ask students to use what they have learned in an original sentence or in rewriting a sentence. *Using What You've Learned,* a two-page lesson at the end of each unit, provides students with an opportunity to "pull together" what they have learned in the unit and apply their learning to a writing situation.

Easy-to-Use Lessons

From the beginning, students feel comfortable with the format of the lessons. Each lesson is introduced with a rule at the top of the page and ends with a meaningful exercise at the bottom of the page. The lessons are clearly labeled, and directions are clear and uncomplicated. Because the format is logical and consistent and the vocabulary is carefully controlled, most students can use *Language Exercises* with a high degree of independence. As the teacher, this allows you the time needed to help students on a one-on-one basis.

Attention to Composition Skills

The process approach to teaching writing provides success for most students. *Language Exercises* provides direct support for the teaching of composition and significantly enhances the strategies and techniques commonly associated with the process-writing approach. Each book includes a composition unit that provides substantial work with important composition skills, such as writing sentences, paragraphs, and letters.

Teacher's Guide

The Teacher's Guide for each level of *Language Exercises* includes a two-page Scope and Sequence chart and an Answer Key in an easy-to-use format for all exercises.

The final section of the Teacher's Guide includes six two-page blackline master Unit Tests presented in a standardized test format. The skills and concepts included on these tests parallel the skills in the end-of-unit Reviews in the student book. These Unit Tests can also be used as both pre- and post-tests. Answers for these tests appear on the final page of the Answer Key.

SCOPE AND SEQUENCE

	A	B	C	D	E	F	G	H	Review
Vocabulary									
Sound Words (Onomatopoeia)	■								
Rhyming Words	■	■							
Synonyms	■	■	■	■	■	■	■	■	■
Antonyms	■	■	■	■	■	■	■	■	■
Homonyms	■	■	■	■	■	■	■	■	■
Multiple Meanings/Homographs	■	■	■	■	■	■	■	■	■
Prefixes and Suffixes			■	■	■	■	■	■	■
Base and Root Words			■	■	■	■	■	■	■
Compound Words			■	■	■	■	■	■	■
Contractions			■	■	■	■	■	■	■
Idioms						■	■	■	■
Connotation/Denotation						■	■	■	■
Sentences									
Word Order in Sentences	■	■							
Recognizing a Sentence	■	■	■	■	■	■	■	■	■
Subjects and Predicates	■	■	■	■	■	■	■	■	■
Types of Sentences	■	■	■	■	■	■	■	■	■
Compound/Complex Sentences			■	■	■	■	■	■	■
Sentence Combining			■	■	■	■	■	■	■
Run-On Sentences				■	■	■	■	■	■
Independent and Subordinate Clauses							■	■	■
Compound Subjects and Predicates						■	■	■	■
Direct and Indirect Objects							■	■	■
Inverted Word Order						■	■	■	■
Grammar and Usage									
Common and Proper Nouns	■	■	■	■	■	■	■	■	■
Singular and Plural Nouns	■	■	■	■	■	■	■	■	■
Possessive Nouns			■	■	■	■	■	■	■
Appositives						■	■	■	■
Verbs	■	■	■	■	■	■	■	■	■
Verb Tense	■	■	■	■	■	■	■	■	■
Regular/Irregular Verbs	■	■	■	■	■	■	■	■	■
Subject/Verb Agreement		■	■	■	■	■	■	■	■
Verb Phrases						■	■	■	■
Transitive and Intransitive Verbs							■	■	■
Verbals: Gerunds, Participles, and Infinitives							■	■	■
Active and Passive Voice							■	■	■
Mood								■	
Pronouns	■	■	■	■	■	■	■	■	■
Antecedents							■	■	■
Articles	■	■	■						
Adjectives	■	■	■	■	■	■	■	■	■
Correct Word Usage (e.g. *may/can, sit/set*)	■	■	■	■	■	■	■	■	■
Adverbs			■	■	■	■	■	■	■
Prepositions						■	■	■	■
Prepositional Phrases						■	■	■	■
Conjunctions						■	■	■	■
Interjections						■	■	■	
Double Negatives								■	■
Capitalization and Punctuation									
Capitalization: First Word in Sentence	■	■	■	■	■	■	■		■
Capitalization: Proper Nouns	■	■	■	■	■	■	■	■	■
Capitalization: in Letters			■	■	■	■	■	■	■
Capitalization: Abbreviations			■	■	■	■	■	■	■
Capitalization: Titles			■	■	■	■	■	■	■

Capitalization and Punctuation (cont'd)	A	B	C	D	E	F	G	H	Review
Capitalization: Proper Adjectives					■	■	■	■	■
End Punctuation	■	■	■	■	■	■	■	■	■
Commas		■	■	■	■	■	■	■	■
Apostrophes in Contractions		■	■	■	■	■	■	■	■
Apostrophes in Possessives			■	■	■	■	■	■	■
Quotation Marks			■	■	■	■	■	■	■
Colons/Semicolons						■	■	■	■
Hyphens						■	■	■	■
Composition									
Expanding Sentences					■	■	■	■	■
Writing a Paragraph		■	■	■	■	■	■	■	■
Paragraphs: Topic Sentence (main idea)		■	■	■	■	■	■	■	■
Paragraphs: Supporting Details		■	■	■	■	■	■	■	■
Order In Paragraphs		■	■	■	■	■	■		■
Writing Process:									
Establishing Purpose		■	■			■	■	■	■
Audience					■	■	■	■	■
Topic		■	■	■	■	■	■	■	■
Outlining				■					
Clustering/Brainstorming					■		■	■	■
Notetaking						■	■		
Revising/Proofreading					■	■	■	■	■
Types of Writing:									
Poem	■								
Letter	■	■	■			■			
"How-to" Paragraph			■						
Invitation			■						
Telephone Message			■						
Conversation				■					
Narrative Paragraph				■					
Comparing and Contrasting					■				
Descriptive Paragraph					■				
Report						■			
Interview							■		
Persuasive Composition								■	■
Readiness/Study Skills									
Grouping	■								
Letters of Alphabet	■								
Listening	■	■							
Making Comparisons	■	■							
Organizing Information	■	■	■						
Following Directions	■	■	■	■	■				
Alphabetical Order	■	■	■	■	■	■	■	■	■
Using a Dictionary:									
Definitions		■	■	■	■	■	■	■	■
Guide Words/Entry Words		■	■	■	■	■	■	■	■
Syllables			■	■	■	■	■		■
Pronunciation			■	■	■	■	■		■
Multiple Meanings				■	■	■	■	■	■
Word Origins						■	■	■	■
Parts of a Book			■	■	■	■	■	■	■
Using the Library						■	■	■	■
Using Encyclopedias				■	■	■	■	■	■
Using Reference Books						■	■	■	■
Using the *Readers' Guide*						■	■	■	■
Using Tables, Charts, Graphs, and Diagrams						■	■	■	■
Choosing Appropriate Sources						■	■	■	■

Answer Key

 Unit 1 Study Skills

Lesson 1, Listening for Directions (P. 1)

Read the following directions to students:

1. Draw a doorknob on the door.
2. Draw a chimney on the roof.
3. Draw smoke coming out of the chimney.
4. Draw a window to the right of the door.
5. Draw a tree beside the left side of the house.
6. Draw a car in the driveway.

Check to see that students have correctly followed your directions.

Lesson 2, More Listening for Directions (P. 2)

Read the following directions to students:

1. Your mother wants you to do a few things when you get home from school. These are her directions: First, make your bed. Then set the table. Finally, feed the cat.
2. Your friend invites you to come to his house. You have never been to his house before. Here are the directions he gives you: Go south on Red Road. Turn west on Green Street. Walk down two houses to 4202 Green Street.
3. Your teacher tells the class about a test. These are his directions: There will be a math test next Friday. It will be at 10:00. It will be on subtraction facts.
4. Your vet wants you to give your dog some medicine. Here are his directions: Give your dog one green pill in the morning. Give your dog a blue pill at noon. Give your dog another green pill in the evening.

Students should write the following key words:

1. 1) make your bed
   2) set the table
   3) feed the cat
2. 1) go south on Red Road
   2) turn west on Green Street
   3) walk down two houses to 4202
3. 1) math test next Friday
   2) 10:00
   3) on subtraction facts
4. 1) one green pill in the morning
   2) a blue pill at noon
   3) another green pill in the evening
5. 1) call 911
   2) tell where you are
   3) describe your emergency

Lesson 3, Following Directions (P. 3)

Check to see that students mark an X in the following places:
1. above
2. on
3. under
4. inside
5. beside, left
6. beside, right

Lesson 4, Following Written Directions (P. 4)

Check to see that students have colored the picture correctly.

Lesson 5, Following Directions to a Place (P. 5)

1. south
2. Fifth Avenue
3. east
4. Main Street
5. 5

Lesson 6, Making Comparisons (P. 6)

1. Robert
2. Sara
3. Robert
4. Sara
5. Robert
6. Sara
7. Sara
8. Robert
9. Sara
10. Robert

Lesson 7, Organizing Information (P. 7)

Top:
Students should cross out the following:
1. turtle
2. dog
3. elephant
4. frog
5. sister
6. popcorn
7. candle
8. mud
9. cry
10. blue

Bottom:

Colors	Names	Actions
red	Andy	eat
blue	Jenny	sing
yellow	Dennis	write
green	Lupe	dance
orange	Rudy	skip
pink	Vince	talk

Lesson 8, Letters in ABC Order (P. 8)

Check students' work for all letters from E to Z.

1. U   7. X
2. J   8. G
3. D   9. Z
4. R   10. Q
5. O   11. F
6. M   12. L

1. K
2. F
3. R
4. G
5. X
6. D
7. U
8. N
9. T
10. B
11. M
12. E

1. A
2. S
3. M
4. W
5. I
6. E
7. K
8. G
9. P
10. R
11. U
12. J

Lesson 9, Words in ABC Order (P. 9)

1. 2, 1, 3   air, bat, cat
2. 3, 2, 1   rock, sea, top
3. 2, 3, 1   dog, egg, fish
4. 2, 3, 1   gate, hat, ice
5. 1, 3, 2   joke, king, lake
6. 2, 3, 1   mail, neck, owl
7. 3, 1, 2   us, very, well
8. 2, 3, 1   X-ray, yes, zoo
9. 3, 2, 1   nail, oak, pan
10. 1, 3, 2   quack, rug, sun

Lesson 10, Finding Words in a Dictionary (P. 10)

Top:
1. baby
2. bed

Bottom:
1. see / sit
2. fit / fun
3. race / run
4. fit / fun
5. race / run
6. see / sit

Lesson 11, Using a Dictionary (P. 11)

1. middle
2. paw
3. open
4. noise
5. many
6. neighbor
7. to go back
8. never used before

Lesson 11, Using a Dictionary (P. 12)

1. no
2. yes
3. no
4. yes
5. no
6. yes
7. yes
8. no
9. no
10. no

Lesson 12, More Than One Meaning (P. 13)

Top:
Students should circle the words in bold.
1. **not warm**
2. a sickness of the nose and throat

1. **to fasten together with string**
2. a cloth worn around the neck

1. **moving water**
2. to move the hands back and forth as a greeting

Bottom:
1. tie   1   3. wave   1   5. cold   1
2. tie   2   4. wave   2   6. cold   2

Lesson 13, Table of Contents (P. 14)

1. Pets
2. 21
3. 7
4. 15
5. Fish
6. Rabbits
7. 7
8. 34
9. Dogs
10. Birds

Review (P. 15)

Read the following directions to students:
Top:
1. Mark an X on the 2. Color the 7 red. Draw a circle around the 4.
2. Color the apple red. Mark an X above the grapes. Draw a banana in the space beside the grapes.

Middle:
1. Your father asks you to help him with the garden. Here are his directions: First, pull the weeds. Then water the plants. Last, pick some flowers.
2. Your teacher asks you to write a report about snakes. Here are her directions: First, find a book about snakes. Then read the book and take notes. Finally, use your notes to write a report.

Top:
Check to see that students have followed your directions.

Middle:
1. 1) pull the weeds
   2) water the plants
   3) pick some flowers
2. 1) find a book about snakes
   2) read the book and take notes
   3) use your notes to write a report

Bottom:
1. south
2. April Drive
3. 3

Review (P. 16)

Students should cross out the following words:
1. help
2. jump

1. 1, 3, 2   almost, hot, peanut
2. 3, 2, 1   teach, you, zoo
3. 2, 1, 3   and, point, town
4. 1, 2, 3   track, voice, wear

1. joke
2. hard

1. poor
2. orange

Using What You've Learned (P. 17)

Top:
Read the following directions to students:
1. Mark an X on the glass of milk.
2. Color the apple red.
3. Draw a sandwich on the plate.

Top:
Check to see that students have followed your directions.

Middle:
Students should do the following:
1. write milk to the right of the glass
2. color the peanut butter brown
3. color the jelly purple
4. circle the knife

Bottom:

Foods	Kitchen Items
peanut butter	knife
jelly	plate
bread	glass

Using What You've Learned (P. 18)

Top:
1. 2
2. 1

Middle:
1. Toys
2. 13
3. 32
4. Balls
5. Games

Bottom:
1. airplane   2. goat
   bake   lake
   dish   moon
   face   pond

 Unit 2 **Vocabulary**

Lesson 14, Words That Rhyme (P. 19)

Top:
1. hop
2. ring
3. door
4. dish
5. ship
6. duck

Bottom:
1. coat
2. rug
3. tree
4. box
5. truck
6. wig

Lesson 15, Words That Mean the Same (P. 20)

1. road
2. home
3. sad
4. sick
5. gift
6. small
7. large
8. dog
9. yell
10. great
11. dad
12. sleep

Lesson 16, Words That Mean the Opposite (P. 21)

Top:
1. soft
2. long
3. dark
4. on
5. happy
6. low

Bottom:
1. dry
2. slow
3. bad
4. cold
5. go
6. hard
7. dirty
8. no

Lesson 17, Words That Sound the Same (P. 22)

Top:
1. hear
2. here
3. here
4. hear
5. here
6. here

Bottom:
1. their
2. their
3. there
4. their
5. there

Lesson 18, More Words That Sound the Same (P. 23)

Top:
1. write
2. right
3. right
4. write
5. right
6. write
7. write
8. right
9. right
10. write
11. right

Bottom:
Sentences will vary.

Lesson 19, Other Words That Sound the Same (P. 24)

1. to
2. two
3. to
4. to
5. too
6. two
7. too
8. too
9. to
10. too
11. to
12. two
13. too
14. to

Lesson 20, Words That Have Two Meanings (P. 25)

1. a
2. b
3. a
4. a
5. a
6. b
7. b
8. a
9. a
10. a
11. b
12. a

Review (P. 26)

1. horn
2. cat
3. bike
4. shed
5. get
6. lake

fed
like
rake
net
corn
mat

1. A
2. A
3. S
4. S
5. A
6. A
7. A
8. S

1. road
2. small
3. yell
4. mom

1. dry
2. easy
3. sour
4. happy

Review (P. 27)

Top:
1. their
2. hear
3. here
4. hear
5. there
6. too
7. to
8. write
9. two
10. right

Bottom:
1. a
2. b
3. b
4. a

Using What You've Learned (P. 28)

Top:
1. Walk up the stairs.
2. Take two big (or large) steps.
3. Open the door.
4. Turn on the light.
5. Find the new shirt.
6. Find a small (or little) box in the pocket.

Bottom:
Answers will vary.

Using What You've Learned (P. 29)

July 5, 1994

Dear Mom and Dad,
  Hear I am in Florida. Grandma wanted me too right a letter two you.
  There are many of Grandma's friends hear. They tell me many stories. I like to here there stories.
  I'll see you in too weeks.

Love,
Randy

July 5, 1994

Dear Mom and Dad,
  Here I am in Florida. Grandma wanted me to write a letter to you.
  There are many of Grandma's friends here. They tell me many stories. I like to hear their stories.
  I'll see you in two weeks.

Love,
Randy

 Unit 3 Sentences

Lesson 21, Sentences (P. 30)

1. no		9. yes
2. yes		10. yes
3. no		11. yes
4. yes		12. no
5. yes		13. yes
6. yes		14. no
7. no		15. no
8. no		16. yes

Lesson 22, More Sentences (P. 31)

Top:
1. Mrs. Brown lives on my street.
2. Our building is made of wood.
3. Four families live in our building.
4. Our school went on a picnic.
5. Jennifer was climbing the tree.
6. The sun shone all day.
7. Corn and beans grow on a farm.
8. The wagon has a broken wheel.
9. The mother goat fed the baby goat.
10. The boat sailed in strong winds.
11. The fisher caught seven fish.
12. Some of the fish were sold in the store.
13. Our team won ten games.
14. Our batters hit the ball a lot.
15. The ballpark was full of fans.

Bottom:
Sentences will vary. Check for completeness.

Lesson 23, Word Order in Sentences (P. 32)

1. My brother eats apples.
2. Elizabeth drinks milk.
3. Kim likes peanut butter.
4. Justin wants bread.
5. Chris plants corn.
6. Chang caught a fish.
7. Dad cooks breakfast.
8. Shawn shares his lunch.
9. Rosa grew the carrot.
10. Kate looks at the pie.

Lesson 24, Telling Sentences (P. 33)

The following sentences are telling sentences:
1, 2, 4, 5, 7, 8, 10, 12, 14, 15

Lesson 25, Asking Sentences (P. 34)

The following sentences are asking sentences:
1, 2, 4, 6, 7, 9, 10, 11, 13, 15

Lesson 26, Kinds of Sentences (P. 35)

Top:

1. asking		6. asking
2. telling		7. telling
3. asking		8. telling
4. telling		9. asking
5. telling		10. asking

Bottom:

Telling Sentences	**Asking Sentences**
I went to the toy store.	Which toy do you want?
I picked a game.	Are there any puzzles?

Lesson 27, Naming Part of Sentences (P. 36)

Students should circle the following parts of each sentence:

1. My family and I		10. Mr. Wolf
2. Sally Harper		11. Sammy Taft
3. Miss Jenkins		12. Mr. O'Dowd
4. Mr. Olson		13. Nina
5. Henry		14. Some children
6. Mr. Byrne		15. Mrs. Clark
7. Mrs. Lee		16. Carolyn and Albert
8. Mr. and Mrs. Diaz		17. Julie
9. Jeanine		

Lesson 28, Action Part of Sentences (P. 37)

Students should circle the following parts of each sentence:

1. live on a busy street		10. brings the mail
2. found a bird		11. brings the paper
3. drives very slowly		12. cooks dinner
4. walks his dog		13. paints the house
5. throws to his dog		14. plant a garden
6. cuts his grass		15. washes her windows
7. picks up her children		16. plant flower seeds
8. shop for food		17. waters the garden
9. plays in the park		

Lesson 29, Sentence Parts (P. 38)

Top:
1. Lions
2. Zebras
3. A pig
4. A cat
5. My dog
6. Fish
7. Birds

Middle:
1. fly
2. buzz
3. barks
4. quack
5. hops
6. roar
7. moo

Bottom:
Sentences will vary.

Review (P. 39)

Top:
1. N
2. S
3. S
4. N

Middle:
1. Alan and Ellen — play on the same team.
2. The big game — is fun to watch.
3. Their coach — teaches them how to play.
4. The phone — rings.
5. Our uncle — is calling from Toronto.
6. Betty and Tom — rush to answer it.
7. The hungry frog — ate an insect.
8. Twenty geese — flew south for the winter.
9. A beetle — is Saturday night.

Bottom:
1. I have a best friend.
2. We ride our bikes together.
3. Sometimes we climb trees.

Review (P. 40)

Top:
1. asking
2. asking
3. telling
4. not a sentence
5. not a sentence
6. telling
7. telling
8. asking
9. not a sentence
10. telling
11. not a sentence
12. asking

Bottom:
1. Many children do chores after school.
2. Mandy and Jeff are good friends.
3. Mandy cleans her room.
4. Jeff walks his dog.

Using What You've Learned (P. 41)

The following sentences should be circled and then written:
1. What is your job?
2. Why do you fly an airplane?
3. Are you scared in the air?
4. Do people have fun on an airplane?
5. How old must you be to fly an airplane?
6. Do you meet any important people?

Using What You've Learned (P. 42)

Top:
1. A big airport is a busy place.
2. Many airplanes are very big.
3. The people on airplanes wear seat belts.
4. A pilot flies the airplane.
5. Many airport workers work very hard.

Bottom:
1. The pilot is my friend.
2. She flies around the world.
3. She sees many countries.
4. I sat in the pilot's seat.
5. The airport is very big.
6. It is easy to get lost.
7. I would like to fly.

 Unit 4 Grammar and Usage

Lesson 30, Naming Words (P. 43)

Top:
1. apple
2. bird
3. boy
4. car
5. chair
6. desk
7. girl
8. grass
9. pen
10. rug
11. tree
12. truck

Bottom:
1. The girl eats an apple.   girl, apple
2. A bird flies to the tree.   bird, tree
3. A chair is by the desk.   chair, desk
4. A boy sits in the chair.   boy, chair
5. The girl plays with a truck.   girl, truck
6. The truck is on the rug.   truck, rug

Lesson 31, Special Naming Words (P. 44)

Top:
1. Bob's Bikes
2. Bridge Road
3. China

4. Elf Corn
5. Gabriel
6. Linda
7. New York City
8. Ohio
9. Pat Green
10. State Street

Bottom:
1. I bought apples at Hill's Store.   Hill's Store
2. The store is on Baker Street.   Baker Street
3. It is near Stone Library.   Stone Library
4. I gave an apple to Emily Fuller.   Emily Fuller

Lesson 32, One and More Than One (P. 45)

Top:
1. caps
2. chairs
3. girls
4. trees
5. flags
6. boys

Middle:
1. lunches
2. dresses
3. glasses
4. dishes
5. boxes
6. watches

Bottom:
1. ponds
2. pigs
3. brushes
4. frogs
5. wishes
6. benches
7. axes
8. balls

Lesson 33, Action Words (P. 46)

Top:
1. The boy reads.
2. The baby cries.
3. The rabbit hops.
4. The birds sing.
5. The dogs bark.

Bottom:
1. runs   8. talks
2. kicks   9. sends
3. breaks   10. talks
4. looks   11. pays
5. shakes   12. shakes
6. turns   13. plays
7. runs

Lesson 34, Naming Word or Action Word (P. 47)

1. class, room
2. teacher, stories
3. stories, elephants
4. Elephants, animals

Middle:
1. takes
2. put
3. rub
4. wash
5. pour

Bottom:
1. verb
2. noun
3. noun
4. verb
5. noun
6. verb
7. noun
8. verb
9. noun

Lesson 35, Adding *-ed* or *-ing* to Verbs (P. 48)

Top:
1. played   6. played
2. called   7. laughing
3. wanted   8. playing
4. laughed   9. watching
5. jumped   10. talking

Bottom:
1. Carmen is finishing her work now.
2. Carmen helped Grandma cook yesterday.
3. Grandma is cooking some soup today.

Lesson 36, Using *Is* or *Are* (P. 49)

Top:
1. are
2. is
3. are
4. is
5. are
6. are
7. are
8. is
9. are

Bottom:
Sentences will vary.

Lesson 37, Using *Was* or *Were* (P. 50)

Top:
1. were
2. was
3. were
4. were
5. were

6. was
7. was
8. were
9. was

Bottom:
Sentences will vary.

Lesson 38, Using *See, Sees,* or *Saw* (P. 51)

Top:
1. sees
2. saw
3. sees
4. sees
5. saw
6. saw
7. see
8. saw
9. saw
10. see

Bottom:
1. saw   Last week we saw Lee.
2. sees   Lee sees my painting now.

Lesson 39, Using *Run, Runs,* or *Ran* (P. 52)

1. ran   Horses ran wild long ago.
2. run   A horse can run ten miles every day.
3. run   Can you run as fast as a horse?
4. ran   Mandy ran in a race last week.
5. runs   Andy runs home from school now.
6. runs   Now Mandy runs after Andy.
7. run   How far can you run?

Lesson 40, Using *Give, Gives,* or *Gave* (P. 53)

Top:
1. give
2. gave
3. gives
4. gave
5. gave
6. gave
7. gave
8. gave
9. gives
10. give

Bottom:
Sentences will vary.

Lesson 41, Using *Do* or *Does* (P. 54)

Top:
1. do
2. does
3. does
4. does
5. does
6. do
7. does
8. do
9. does
10. do
11. do
12. do

Bottom:
Sentences will vary.

Lesson 42, Using *Has, Have,* or *Had* (P. 55)

1. had
2. has
3. have
4. have
5. has
6. had
7. has
8. has
9. have
10. had
11. had
12. has
13. had
14. had

Lesson 43, Pronouns (P. 56)

1. She got a gift.
2. It was for her birthday.
3. He brought the gift.
4. They found a box.
5. We are going to the party.
6. They will wear hats.
7. She likes punch.
8. It will end soon.

Lesson 44, Using *I* or *Me* (P. 57)

Top:
1. I
2. I
3. me
4. me
5. I
6. I

Bottom:
1. I
2. me
3. I
4. I
5. I
6. me
7. I
8. I

Lesson 45, Using *A* or *An* (P. 58)

1. an
2. a
3. a
4. an
5. a
6. an
7. an
8. an
9. a
10. a
11. a
12. a
13. an
14. an
15. a
16. a
17. a
18. an
19. an
20. a
21. an
22. an
23. an
24. a

Lesson 46, Using Words That Compare (P. 59)

1. younger   Dad is younger than Mom.
2. oldest   Kim is the oldest of four children.
3. smaller   An ant is smaller than a pig.
4. longest   That snake is the longest of the six at the zoo.
5. taller   The barn is taller than the house.
6. stronger   Alex is stronger than Michael.
7. softest   That blue chair is the softest in the room.

Review (P. 60)

Students should circle the nouns and underline the verbs.

Nouns	Verbs
1. children, beach	play
2. sand, feet	hurts
3. Boats, waves	float

1. Mr. Harper
2. Colorado
3. Tom Adams Drive
4. Granger Park

1. dresses
2. boxes
3. trees
4. foxes

1. opening
2. pulled
3. playing
4. jumped
5. looking

Review (P. 61)

1. is
2. were
3. a
4. has
5. runs
6. gave
7. I
8. an
9. biggest

1. see
2. saw
3. do
4. does

1. We went to a movie.
2. They said it was a good movie.
3. She wants to see it again.
4. He wants to go again next week.

Using What You've Learned (P. 62)

John: Janet and I are twins.
Janet: We were born on the same day.
John: I am older than Janet. I was born one minute before Janet. Our brother James is the oldest of all the children.
Janet: Mom was surprised when she saw us. She was not ready for two babies.

John: Dad was surprised when he saw two of us, too.
John: After we were born, Dad ran to the telephone.
Janet: He called Grandma.
John: He said, "Do you believe this? Now we have two babies!"

Using What You've Learned (P. 63)

Once upon a time there were many wolves. The wolves tried to catch the sheep. The people who watched the sheep had a meeting. They said, "If you see a wolf, shout 'Wolf, wolf!' Then we can help you scare the wolf away."

One boy wanted to play a funny joke on the others. He waited until the people were asleep. The boy cried, "Wolf, wolf!"

All the people ran to help him. But no wolf was there. The people were angry. They said, "You have played a trick on us."

The next night a wolf came. The boy cried, "Wolf, wolf!"

But no one ran to help the boy. The people thought it was another trick. The boy lost all his sheep to the wolf.

 **Unit 5**   **Capitalization and Punctuation**

Lesson 47, Writing Names of People (P. 64)

Top:
1. Mark Twain
2. Bill Clinton
3. Roy Mayers
4. Michael Jordan
5. Leslie Ford

Middle:
Students should circle the first letter of the following:
1. mother, grandma
2. grandma, grandpa
3. uncle carlos, aunt kathy

Bottom:
1. Did Dad help Mom?
2. Grandma and I played ball.
3. Uncle Frank is visiting us.

Lesson 48, Writing Initials (P. 65)

Top:
1. R. L.
2. C. A. C.
3. M. B.
4. M. B.
5. C. F.
6. T. L. T.
7. I. B.
8. L. A. W.

Middle:
1. J. W. A.
2. L. B. Hopkins
3. J. Yolen
4. P. A. R.

Bottom:
1. The box was for M. S. Mills.
2. D. E. Ellis sent it to her.
3. T. J. Lee brought the box to the house.

Lesson 49, Writing Titles of Respect (P. 66)

Top:
1. Mrs. Ruth Scott
2. Mr. Kurt Wiese
3. Miss E. Garcia
4. Dr. Seuss
5. Ms. Carol Baylor
6. Mr. and Mrs. H. Cox
7. Miss K. E. Jones

Bottom:
1. Mrs. H. Stone is here to see Dr. Brooks.
2. Dr. Brooks and Ms. Miller are not here.
3. Miss Ari and Mr. Lee came together.
4. Mr. F. Green will go in first.

Lesson 50, Writing Names of Places (P. 67)

Top:
1. James lives on Market Street.
2. I think Thomas Park is in this town.
3. We went to Mathis Lake for a picnic.
4. Is Seton School far away?

Bottom:
1. Webb St.
2. Airport Rd.
3. Doe Dr.
4. Hill Rd.
5. Bell St.
6. Oak Dr.

Lesson 51, Writing Names of Days (P. 68)

Top:
1. Sunday
2. Friday
3. Wednesday
4.-5. Answers will vary.

Bottom:
1. Sunday   Sun.
2. Monday   Mon.
3. Tuesday   Tues.
4. Wednesday   Wed.
5. Thursday   Thurs.
6. Friday   Fri.
7. Saturday   Sat.

Lesson 52, Writing Names of Months (P. 69)

Top:
1. January   7. July
2. February   8. August
3. March   9. September
4. April   10. October
5. May   11. November
6. June   12. December

Bottom:
1. Jan.
2. Mar.
3. Nov.
4. Aug.
5. Sept.
6. Feb.
7. Oct.
8. Dec.
9. Apr.

Lesson 53, Writing Names of Seasons (P. 70)

Top:

winter	spring	summer	fall
December	March	June	September
January	April	July	October
February	May	August	November

Bottom:
1. winter
2. spring
3. summer
4. fall

Lesson 54, Writing Names of Holidays (P. 71)

Top:
1. New Year's Day
2. Mother's Day
3. Independence Day
4. Labor Day
5. Victoria Day
6. Thanksgiving Day

Bottom:
1. January 1 is New Year's Day.
2. I like Valentine's Day.
3. Boxing Day is a British holiday.
4. Father's Day is in June.
5. Thanksgiving is on Thursday.
6. We have a picnic on Independence Day.

Lesson 55, Writing Book Titles (P. 72)

1. The Doorbell Rang
2. Best Friends
3. Rabbits on Roller Skates
4. The Cat in the Hat
5. Down on the Sunny Farm
6. Fifty Saves His Friend
7. Goodbye House
8. The Biggest Bear

Lesson 56, Beginning Sentences (P. 73)

1. Deb likes to play ball.
2. Her ball is red.
3. Jet wants to play.
4. Jet likes the ball.
5. Deb throws the ball.

6. The ball goes far.
7. Jet runs to the ball.
8. Jet brings the ball back.
9. Deb hugs her dog.
10. They have fun together.

Lesson 57, Ending Sentences (P. 74)

Top:
1. Patty played on the baseball team.
2. She played hard.
3. She hit two home runs.

Bottom:
1. What time is it?
2. Is it time for lunch?
3. Are you ready to eat?
4. Do you like apples?

Lesson 58, Using Commas in Lists (P. 75)

Top:
1. We go to school on Monday, Tuesday, Wednesday, Thursday, and Friday.
2. We draw, sing, and read on Monday.
3. Our class went to the post office, the firehouse, and the zoo.
4. We ran, jumped, laughed, and ate at the zoo.
5. Elephants, lions, tigers, and bears live at the zoo.

Bottom:
1. Pam, Kay, and Juan work hard.
2. Pam sings, dances, and acts in the play.
3. Kay cleans, fixes, and paints the stage.

Lesson 59, Using Commas in Place Names (P. 76)

Top:
1. Akron, Ohio
2. Hilo, Hawaii
3. Macon, Georgia
4. Nome, Alaska
5. Provo, Utah

Bottom:
1. Nancy lives in Barnet, Vermont.
2. Mr. Hill went to Houston, Texas.
3. Did Bruce like Bend, Oregon?
4. Will Amy visit Newark, Ohio?
5. How far away is Salem, Maine?

Lesson 60, Using Commas in Dates (P. 77)

Top:
1. Dec. 12, 1948
2. Mar. 27, 1965
3. Sept. 8, 1994
4. Nov. 1, 1999
5. Jan. 5, 1995

Bottom:
1. Jim was born on August 10, 1967.
2. Jen's birthday is Oct. 17, 1983.
3. Maria visited on February 8, 1991.
4. Dad's party was on July 29, 1989.
5. Carrie starts school on Sept. 3, 1991.
6. My library books go back on March 17, 1990.
7. Luis lost his first tooth on Oct. 20, 1988.
8. Answers will vary.

Lesson 61, Using Apostrophes in Contractions (P. 78)

Top:
1. were not — wasn't
2. was not — weren't
3. has not — haven't
4. have not — hasn't
5. did not — didn't
6. are not — aren't

Middle:
1. is not
2. do not
3. was not
4. can not
5. did not
6. had not
7. does not
8. are not

Bottom:
1. isn't
2. don't
3. didn't
4. wasn't
5. weren't

Review (P. 79)

Students should circle the first letter of the following:
1. grandpa, speedy
2. our, tippy, mittens
3. david, fluff
4. grandma, grandpa, fluff

1. Mr. W. Bell didn't work on Friday.
2. June isn't a winter month.
3. Is Thanksgiving in November?
4. Wasn't Ms. E. Smith going to be in the Earth Day parade?

1. Fifth St.
2. Red River Rd.
3. Adams Dr.

1. Mon.   4. Tues.
2. Wed.   5. Fri.
3. Sat.   6. Thurs.

Review (P. 80)

1. July 4, 1990
2. Sept. 5, 1991
3. Jan. 20, 1993
4. Apr. 1, 1994

1. The Princess and the Pea
2. Once a Mouse

1. Trina jumped, ran, and swam to win first place.
2. The seasons are winter, spring, summer, and fall.
3. Dionne lives in Seattle, Washington.
4. This letter is going to Chicago, Illinois.

1. weren't
2. hasn't
3. aren't
4. don't
5. wasn't
6. isn't

Using What You've Learned (P. 81)

Answers will vary.

Using What You've Learned (P. 82)

Answers will vary.

Unit 6 Composition

Lesson 62, Writing Sentences (P. 83)

Top, Middle, and Bottom:
Sentences will vary.

Lesson 63, Paragraphs (P. 84)

Top:
1. Charise
2. Charise is studying for her math test.

Bottom:
1. My sister's birthday
2. Today is my sister's birthday.

Lesson 64, Main Idea (P. 85)

1. Uncle Joe is a funny man.
2. Dad told us a funny story about his dog.
3. Firefighters are brave people.

Lesson 65, Supporting Details (P. 86)

Students should circle the first sentence in each paragraph and underline all the other sentences.

Lesson 66, Order in Paragraphs (P. 87)

Top:	Bottom:
3	2
2	3
4	4
1	1

Lesson 67, Parts of a Letter (P. 88)

Tell students to fill in the current year.
1. Chris
2. Rose
3. 608 Weston Dr., Markham, Ontario L3R 1E5

Lesson 68, Planning a Letter (P. 89)

Answers will vary.

Lesson 69, Writing a Friendly Letter (P. 90)

Tell students to fill in the current year.

> 711 Short St.
> Bluff, Utah 84512
> Oct. 17, 19___

Dear Pat,
   I just found out some good news. We are moving in June! I will still go to camp in July. I will see you then.
> Your friend,
> Anna Gomez

Lesson 70, Writing Addresses (P. 91)

Return address:	Address:
Miss Anna Gomez	Ms. Pat Murray
711 Short Street	704 Heard Road
Bluff, Utah 84512	Akron, Ohio 44309

Review (P. 92)

Top and Middle:
Answers will vary.

Bottom:
1. two girls who wanted to go to a movie
2. Lauren and Yuko wanted to go to a movie.

Review (P. 93)

Top:
Students should circle the following sentence. All other sentences should be underlined.
I really want a dog.

Bottom:
Tell students to write in the current year. Students should circle the letters in bold.

> 112 Maplewood St.
> Cedarburg, Wisconsin 53012 } heading
> Oct. 20, 19___

greeting → **d**ear **a**unt **j**ulie,
>   I was picked to be on the Padres' baseball team. Dad is going to help me. We have been playing catch in the yard. } body
>   I can't wait to start playing in June. Can you come and watch me play?
>   with love, ←————— closing
>   Terry ←————— name

Using What You've Learned (P. 94)

Letters will vary.

Using What You've Learned (P. 95)

Answers will vary.

Final Reviews

Final Review, Unit 1 (P. 96)

Top:
Read the following directions to students:
1. Put an X on the sea horse.
2. Draw a circle around the plant to the left of the rocks.
3. Color the sand yellow.

Check to see that students have correctly followed the directions.

Middle:
1. Metric Avenue
2. Park Street
3. 2

Bottom:
Students should cross out the following words:
1. flag
2. bark
3. flower
4. book

Final Review, Unit 1 (P. 97)

1. 2, 3, 1   angry, chair, hot
2. 1, 3, 2   nest, off, penny

1. poor, quack
2. really, pair

1. broken
2. baby
3. the day someone was born

1. forts and castles
2. 12
3. 34

Final Review, Unit 2 (P. 98)

1. hold	13. their
2. boat	14. There
3. pat	15. there
4. dirty	16. right
5. slow	17. write
6. hard	18. right
7. glad	19. two
8. ill	20. to
9. shout	21. to
10. hear	22. too
11. here	23. two
12. here	

Final Review, Unit 2 (P. 99)

1. a
2. b
3. a
4. a
5. b
6. a
7. a
8. b
9. b
10. a
11. a
12. b
13. b
14. b
15. a

Final Review, Unit 3 (P. 100)

Top:
1. yes
2. no
3. yes
4. no
5. yes
6. no

Middle:
1. Milk was on the table.
2. Butter comes from milk.
3. Cheese also comes from milk.
4. Joanna likes to drink milk.
5. Brad spilled his milk.

Bottom:
1. A
2. T
3. T
4. A
5. T
6. A
7. T
8. T

Final Review, Unit 3 (P. 101)

Top:
1. My family works together to clean the house.
2. Phillip dusts the bookshelves in his room.
3. Katie and Kathy do the laundry.
4. The dirty dishes need to be washed.
5. The house looks very clean now.

Middle:
1. The orange tastes sweet.
2. A lemon smells sour.
3. The sandpaper feels rough.
4. That baby sounds angry.
5. The painting looks better over the table.

Bottom:
Students should circle the words in bold.
1. **Our class** surprised Miss Muller.
2. **All the children** brought flowers.
3. **Sarah and Shawn** put them in a glass.
4. **Some children** made cards for Miss Muller.
5. **The girls and boys** shouted for their teacher.

Final Review, Unit 4 (P. 102)

1. noun
2. verb
3. noun
4. verb

1. Ms. Grayson
2. Atlanta
3. Georgia

1. trees
2. axes
3. classes
4. bushes
5. lunches
6. foxes

1. walked
2. working
3. asked
4. waiting
5. helped

Final Review, Unit 4 (P. 103)

Top:
1. ran
2. was
3. saw
4. had
5. I
6. Are
7. played
8. gave
9. an
10. Do

Bottom:
1. They planned a party.
2. It was for Steve's birthday.
3. She invited the guests.
4. We helped put up balloons.
5. He made the cake.
6. He was very surprised.

Final Review, Unit 5 (P. 104)

Students should circle the letters in bold.
1. **mr. w. c. s**anchez works at **h**arris **s**chool.
2. **mr. k**elly took his class to **r**iverside **p**ark.
3. **t**hey will go to the **h**udson **r**iver in **s**eptember.
4. **w**ill **g**randfather come to see **a**unt **r**uth?
5. **d**id **u**ncle **b**ill come for **t**hanksgiving?
6. **d**onna took a boat ride on **l**ake **e**rie last summer.
7. **d**onna and **i** met **ms. h. m. s**lade last fall.
8. **w**e went to a party for **mrs. l**ee in **n**ovember.

1. March — Mar.
2. is not — isn't
3. December — Dec.
4. Saturday — Sat.
5. January — Jan.
6. Sunday — Sun.
7. do not — don't
8. Wednesday — Wed.

1. Hanson Dr.
2. Baker Rd.
3. Second St.

1. Forts and Castles
2. Babar the King

Final Review, Unit 5 (P. 105)

1. What will you do in Reno, Nevada?
2. Who is with Dr. Trigo?
3. It is Mr. V. F. Casey.
4. He was born on March 20, 1974.
5. He likes to read, dance, and sing.
6. His family moved there on June 4, 1978.
7. I will be out of town in March, April, and May.
8. Did Ms. Kirkpatrick go to San Francisco, California?
9. The parade will be on New Year's Day.
10. Dr. Nguyen will be in town on Nov. 12.
11. How can we get to Santa Fe, New Mexico?
12. Miss Hall will be late on Monday, Wednesday, and Friday.

Final Review, Unit 6 (P. 106)

Top:
Answers will vary.

Middle:
Answers will vary.

Bottom:
Students should circle the sentence in bold and underline the other sentences.
1. **Baseball is a sport I like very much.** I like to play on the city team in the summer. I've been saving baseball cards since I was five. I like to watch games at night. I have a great time at the ballpark.
2. **Puppies like a lot of playtime.** They like to chase balls. They play with people, as well as other dogs. They can play for hours.

Final Review, Unit 6 (P. 107)

Top:
3, 2, 4, 1
Bottom:

Mr. J. T. Conners
4203 Greystone Drive
Cincinnati, Ohio 45236

Marla Franklin
1240 Sunset Road
Denver, Colorado 80919

Tests

TEST: Unit 1, Pages 21–22, Teacher's Guide

1.	C	13.	B
2.	A	14.	A
3.	A	15.	C
4.	B	16.	C
5.	C	17.	C
6.	C	18.	A
7.	B	19.	C
8.	C	20.	B
9.	A	21.	B
10.	B	22.	C
11.	A	23.	A
12.	C	24.	C

TEST: Unit 2, Pages 23–24, Teacher's Guide

1.	A	11.	B
2.	B	12.	B
3.	C	13.	A
4.	B	14.	A
5.	C	15.	B
6.	A	16.	B
7.	A	17.	A
8.	B	18.	A
9.	C	19.	B
10.	A	20.	A

TEST: Unit 3, Pages 25–26, Teacher's Guide

1.	B	19.	A
2.	A	20.	A
3.	B	21.	B
4.	A	22.	A
5.	B	23.	B
6.	B	24.	A
7.	A	25.	B
8.	A	26.	A
9.	B	27.	A
10.	A	28.	B
11.	B	29.	B
12.	B	30.	A
13.	C	31.	B
14.	B	32.	B
15.	A	33.	A
16.	A	34.	B
17.	B	35.	B
18.	C	36.	A

TEST: Unit 4, Pages 27–28, Teacher's Guide

1.	A	21.	A
2.	B	22.	B
3.	A	23.	C
4.	A	24.	C
5.	A	25.	B
6.	B	26.	C
7.	A	27.	B
8.	B	28.	A
9.	A	29.	A
10.	A	30.	B
11.	B	31.	B
12.	A	32.	C
13.	C	33.	C
14.	A	34.	B
15.	B	35.	B
16.	B	36.	B
17.	A	37.	C
18.	A	38.	A
19.	B	39.	A
20.	A	40.	A

TEST: Unit 5, Pages 29–30, Teacher's Guide

1.	A	16.	C
2.	B	17.	C
3.	A	18.	A
4.	B	19.	A
5.	C	20.	A
6.	A	21.	C
7.	B	22.	B
8.	C	23.	C
9.	A	24.	A
10.	A	25.	C
11.	C	26.	C
12.	A	27.	A
13.	B	28.	C
14.	B	29.	B
15.	B		

TEST: Unit 6, Pages 31–32, Teacher's Guide

1.	A
2.	B
3.	C
4.	B
5.	B
6.	C
7.	A
8.	C
9.	B

Choose the apple with an <u>X</u> on it.

1. A ○   B ○   C ○

Choose the train with an <u>X</u> beside it, on the right.

2. A ○    B ○    C ○

Choose the butterfly with a circle around it.

3. A ○   B ○   C ○

Look at the map, and read the directions. Then answer the questions.

Directions to Roberto's House

   1) Go east on Shark Road.
   2) Turn south on Dolphin Drive.
   3) Walk down two houses to 403 Dolphin Drive.

4. What direction do you go first?

   A ○ north   B ○ east   C ○ south

5. How many houses down Dolphin Drive is Roberto's house?

   A ○ 4   B ○ 3   C ○ 2

Name _____

Choose the word that does not belong.

6. A ○ tree   **B** ○ flower   **C** ○ rug   **10. A** ○ boy   **B** ○ cake   **C** ○ man

7. A ○ milk   **B** ○ name   **C** ○ juice   **11. A** ○ pink   **B** ○ car   **C** ○ boat

8. A ○ cup   **B** ○ plate   **C** ○ pen   **12. A** ○ red   **B** ○ blue   **C** ○ swim

9. A ○ ball   **B** ○ cat   **C** ○ dog   **13. A** ○ car   **B** ○ grass   **C** ○ truck

Choose the list that is in ABC order.

14. A ○ bird   **B** ○ dark   **C** ○ bird   **16. A** ○ nine   **B** ○ rest   **C** ○ mill
      dark   king   king   rest   mill   nine
      king   bird   dark   mill   nine   rest

15. A ○ map   **B** ○ zoo   **C** ○ cat   **17. A** ○ door   **B** ○ fun   **C** ○ door
      zoo   cat   map   knob   door   fun
      cat   map   zoo   fun   knob   knob

Choose the word that would be on the same page as the guide words.

day / fish   **joke / lost**

18. A ○ dear   **B** ○ laugh   **C** ○ pig   **21. A** ○ park   **B** ○ key   **C** ○ snow

19. A ○ red   **B** ○ sell   **C** ○ egg   **22. A** ○ today   **B** ○ could   **C** ○ lamp

20. A ○ ball   **B** ○ dog   **C** ○ goat   **23. A** ○ jot   **B** ○ ice   **C** ○ meat

Choose the sentence that goes with definition #1.

24. A ○ I saw a bat at the zoo.

     B ○ Are you afraid of bats?

     C ○ Our team has a new bat.

     D ○ Bats can see at night.

> **bat 1.** a wooden stick used to play baseball
>
> **2.** an animal that flies at night

Choose the correct word to complete each sentence.

1. A word that rhymes with <u>bake</u> is ___.

   A ○ take   **B** ○ goat   **C** ○ cook

2. A word that rhymes with <u>ship</u> is ___.

   A ○ boat   **B** ○ drip   **C** ○ shut

3. <u>Grin</u> means almost the same as ___.

   A ○ pin   **B** ○ cry   **C** ○ smile

4. <u>House</u> means almost the same as ___.

   A ○ trip   **B** ○ home   **C** ○ mouse

5. The opposite of <u>long</u> is ___.

   A ○ song   **B** ○ tall   **C** ○ short

6. The opposite of <u>hot</u> is ___.

   A ○ cold   **B** ○ warm   **C** ○ pot

7. Did you ___ about the prize?

   A ○ hear   **B** ○ here   **C** ○ there

8. Jenna and Chris will bring ___ books to the library.

   A ○ there   **B** ○ their   **C** ○ hear

9. I have learned how to ___ all the spelling words.

   A ○ right   **B** ○ wrote   **C** ○ write

10. Our class wants ___ play outside today.

    A ○ to   **B** ○ too   **C** ○ two

11. I have ___ many books to carry!

    A ○ to   **B** ○ too   **C** ○ two

Name _____ **23**

Look at each pair of pictures. Read each sentence. Then choose the letter of the correct meaning for the underlined word.

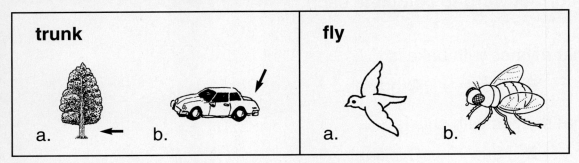

trunk

a.   b.

fly

a.   b.

12. Joanne got the packages out of the <u>trunk</u>.

    A ○ meaning <u>a</u>   **B** ○ meaning <u>b</u>

13. I sat beside the tree and leaned against its <u>trunk</u>.

    A ○ meaning <u>a</u>   **B** ○ meaning <u>b</u>

14. There was a large hole in the <u>trunk</u> of the tree.

    A ○ meaning <u>a</u>   **B** ○ meaning <u>b</u>

15. The spare tire for the car is in the <u>trunk</u>.

    A ○ meaning <u>a</u>   **B** ○ meaning <u>b</u>

16. There is a <u>fly</u> on the wall.

    A ○ meaning <u>a</u>   **B** ○ meaning <u>b</u>

17. Geese usually <u>fly</u> south for the winter.

    A ○ meaning <u>a</u>   **B** ○ meaning <u>b</u>

18. An ostrich is a bird that cannot <u>fly</u>.

    A ○ meaning <u>a</u>   **B** ○ meaning <u>b</u>

19. The <u>fly</u> kept buzzing in my ear.

    A ○ meaning <u>a</u>   **B** ○ meaning <u>b</u>

20. I saw the bird <u>fly</u> to its nest.

    A ○ meaning <u>a</u>   **B** ○ meaning <u>b</u>

Choose whether the group of words is a sentence.

1. Seven children from my class.   **A** ○ yes   **B** ○ no

2. Joe and Margaret are best friends.   **A** ○ yes   **B** ○ no

3. Got here today.   **A** ○ yes   **B** ○ no

4. I can swim.   **A** ○ yes   **B** ○ no

5. Kathy doesn't know if.   **A** ○ yes   **B** ○ no

6. The girls and boys.   **A** ○ yes   **B** ○ no

7. We will walk today.   **A** ○ yes   **B** ○ no

8. Gina studied for the test.   **A** ○ yes   **B** ○ no

9. My father needs.   **A** ○ yes   **B** ○ no

10. Uncle Jeremy is out of town.   **A** ○ yes   **B** ○ no

Choose the sentences that are in an order that makes sense.

11. **A** ○ It time what is?
    B ○ What time is it?
    C ○ Time what it is?

12. **A** ○ Is caught my kite in a tree.
    B ○ My kite is caught in a tree.
    C ○ Tree is a my kite caught is.

13. **A** ○ Tomorrow my birthday is.
    B ○ My is tomorrow birthday.
    C ○ My birthday is tomorrow.

14. **A** ○ Circus the is fun.
    B ○ The circus is fun.
    C ○ Fun the circus is.

15. **A** ○ My sister went to the store.
    B ○ My store went to the sister.
    C ○ To the store my went sister.

16. **A** ○ Tina likes to ride horses.
    B ○ Ride horses Tina likes to.
    C ○ Likes to ride horses Tina.

17. **A** ○ Rang the telephone.
    B ○ The telephone rang.
    C ○ The rang telephone.

18. **A** ○ His Toby plays with puppy.
    B ○ Puppy plays Toby with his.
    C ○ Toby plays with his puppy.

Name _____   **25**

Choose <u>telling</u> or <u>asking</u> for each sentence.

19. Daisy is my dog.　　　　　　　　**A** ○ telling　　**B** ○ asking

20. She can follow directions.　　　　**A** ○ telling　　**B** ○ asking

21. Does she have a doghouse?　　　**A** ○ telling　　**B** ○ asking

22. She stays in our house.　　　　　**A** ○ telling　　**B** ○ asking

23. Where does Daisy play?　　　　　**A** ○ telling　　**B** ○ asking

24. She plays in the yard.　　　　　　**A** ○ telling　　**B** ○ asking

25. What is Daisy doing?　　　　　　**A** ○ telling　　**B** ○ asking

26. Daisy likes to dig in the yard.　　**A** ○ telling　　**B** ○ asking

27. Daisy hid her bone.　　　　　　　**A** ○ telling　　**B** ○ asking

28. Do you know where her bone is?　**A** ○ telling　　**B** ○ asking

Choose <u>naming part</u> or <u>action part</u> to tell about the underlined words in each sentence.

29. Megan <u>studied for her test</u>.　　**A** ○ naming part　**B** ○ action part

30. <u>The children on my street</u> play together.　　**A** ○ naming part　**B** ○ action part

31. My little sister <u>loves to play soccer</u>.　　**A** ○ naming part　**B** ○ action part

32. I <u>will go to school</u>.　　**A** ○ naming part　**B** ○ action part

33. <u>My brother</u> loves to swim.　　**A** ○ naming part　**B** ○ action part

34. Janet's grandparents <u>went to the coast</u>.　　**A** ○ naming part　**B** ○ action part

35. The winner <u>gets a blue ribbon</u>.　　**A** ○ naming part　**B** ○ action part

36. <u>A farmer</u> plants crops.　　**A** ○ naming part　**B** ○ action part

Choose noun or verb for each underlined word.

1. The swimming <u>pool</u> opens today. **A** ○ noun **B** ○ verb

2. I <u>jump</u> in the deep water. **A** ○ noun **B** ○ verb

3. <u>Kenny</u> and I race across the pool. **A** ○ noun **B** ○ verb

4. The <u>water</u> feels cool. **A** ○ noun **B** ○ verb

5. Some of my <u>friends</u> are at the pool. **A** ○ noun **B** ○ verb

6. The pool <u>closes</u> soon. **A** ○ noun **B** ○ verb

Choose whether the underlined words are proper nouns.

7. Is <u>Lisa</u> going to the party? **A** ○ yes **B** ○ no

8. Our whole <u>team</u> is going to the party. **A** ○ yes **B** ○ no

9. The party will be at <u>Pizza Parade</u>. **A** ○ yes **B** ○ no

10. Pizza Parade is on <u>Coral Drive</u>. **A** ○ yes **B** ○ no

11. What <u>day</u> of the week is the party? **A** ○ yes **B** ○ no

12. The party is on <u>Saturday</u>. **A** ○ yes **B** ○ no

Choose the noun that means more than one.

13. **A** ○ bag **B** ○ yard **C** ○ boxes

14. **A** ○ bands **B** ○ engine **C** ○ dog

15. **A** ○ field **B** ○ lunches **C** ○ dollar

16. **A** ○ fire **B** ○ ovens **C** ○ class

17. **A** ○ foxes **B** ○ puddle **C** ○ sky

18. **A** ○ glasses **B** ○ pond **C** ○ flag

Name _____ 27

Choose the correct word to complete each sentence.

19. Where ___ the ducks go?   **A** ○ does   **B** ○ do   **C** ○ fly

20. Do you wear ___ watch?   **A** ○ a   **B** ○ an   **C** ○ two

21. The squirrel ___ up into the tree.   **A** ○ ran   **B** ○ run   **C** ○ fast

22. The boy said ___ would be back.   **A** ○ me   **B** ○ he   **C** ○ our

23. Our friends ___ at school.   **A** ○ is   **B** ○ was   **C** ○ were

24. I was ___ by the tree.   **A** ○ wait   **B** ○ waited   **C** ○ waiting

25. Dan and ___ played catch.   **A** ○ me   **B** ○ I   **C** ○ him

26. Can Peter borrow ___ ?   **A** ○ we   **B** ○ she   **C** ○ it

27. The band ___ beautiful music.   **A** ○ play   **B** ○ played   **C** ○ playing

28. ___ has a part in the play.   **A** ○ She   **B** ○ We   **C** ○ Me

29. Did you bring ___ apple?   **A** ○ an   **B** ○ a   **C** ○ two

30. This orange is ___ than that one.   **A** ○ sweet   **B** ○ sweeter   **C** ○ sweetest

31. You ___ finished working.   **A** ○ is   **B** ○ are   **C** ○ was

32. I do not know who ___ are.   **A** ○ I   **B** ○ he   **C** ○ they

33. I ___ the dog last week.   **A** ○ sees   **B** ○ see   **C** ○ saw

34. Do ___ need anything at the store?   **A** ○ me   **B** ○ we   **C** ○ us

35. They ___ us now!   **A** ○ sees   **B** ○ see   **C** ○ saw

36. I hope that present is for ___ .   **A** ○ I   **B** ○ me   **C** ○ they

37. He ___ you his chair.   **A** ○ giving   **B** ○ give   **C** ○ gave

38. They ___ nice friends.   **A** ○ have   **B** ○ has   **C** ○ do

39. He always ___ me a smile.   **A** ○ gives   **B** ○ give   **C** ○ does

40. That is the ___ frog I've ever seen!   **A** ○ biggest   **B** ○ bigger   **C** ○ big

Choose the sentence with the correct capital letters.

1. **A** ○ Mrs. Fuller drove to Byrne Park.
    B ○ mrs. fuller drove to Byrne Park.
    C ○ Mrs. Fuller drove to byrne park.

2. **A** ○ aunt julie visited elm school.
    B ○ Aunt Julie visited Elm School.
    C ○ aunt Julie visited elm school.

3. **A** ○ Dr. A. Hanson is here.
    B ○ Dr. a. hanson is here.
    C ○ dr. A. Hanson is here.

4. **A** ○ next monday is a holiday.
    B ○ Next Monday is a holiday.
    C ○ Next monday is a Holiday.

5. **A** ○ School Starts in the Fall.
    B ○ school starts in the fall.
    C ○ School starts in the fall.

6. **A** ○ I made a card for Father's Day.
    B ○ i made a card for father's day.
    C ○ I made a card for father's Day.

7. **A** ○ It snowed last january.
    B ○ It snowed last January.
    C ○ it snowed last January.

8. **A** ○ Turn left on Fifth street.
    B ○ Turn left on fifth street.
    C ○ Turn left on Fifth Street.

9. **A** ○ Carlos flew to Austin, Texas.
    B ○ Carlos flew to austin, texas.
    C ○ carlos flew to Austin, Texas.

10. **A** ○ J. I. Ross met R. P. Cain.
    B ○ j. i. Ross met r. p. Cain.
    C ○ J. I. ross met R. P. cain.

Choose the book title with the correct capital letters.

11. **A** ○ Water life
    B ○ water life
    C ○ Water Life

12. **A** ○ Language Exercises
    B ○ language Exercises
    C ○ Language exercises

13. **A** ○ Voices from world history
    B ○ Voices from World History
    C ○ voices From world history

14. **A** ○ protecting wildlife
    B ○ Protecting Wildlife
    C ○ protecting Wildlife

Choose the correct short form for each word.

15. December   **A** ○ Decem.   **B** ○ Dec.   **C** ○ Dcbr.

16. cannot   **A** ○ cant'   **B** ○ can'ot   **C** ○ can't

17. Monday   **A** ○ Mond.   **B** ○ mo.   **C** ○ Mon.

18. Street   **A** ○ St.   **B** ○ Strt.   **C** ○ Str.

19. do not   **A** ○ don't   **B** ○ do'nt   **C** ○ d'ont

20. was not   **A** ○ wasn't   **B** ○ wasnt'   **C** ○ was'nt

21. have not   **A** ○ hav'nt   **B** ○ havnt'   **C** ○ haven't

22. Friday   **A** ○ Fr.   **B** ○ Fri.   **C** ○ fri

23. August   **A** ○ Agst.   **B** ○ Ag.   **C** ○ Aug.

24. Tuesday   **A** ○ Tues.   **B** ○ Tue   **C** ○ Tu.

25. are not   **A** ○ areno't   **B** ○ arn't   **C** ○ aren't

Choose the sentence with the correct periods, question marks, and commas.

26. **A** ○ Mr. J. Garcia was born on Oct 17 1965.
    B ○ Mr J Garcia was born on Oct. 17 1965.
    C ○ Mr. J. Garcia was born on Oct. 17, 1965.

27. **A** ○ Where was Dr. Blair on Apr. 12, 1989?
    B ○ Where was Dr. Blair on Apr. 12, 1989.
    C ○ Where was Dr Blair on Apr 12 1989?

28. **A** ○ Did you play on Dove St. last night.
    B ○ Did you play on Dove St last night?
    C ○ Did you play on Dove St. last night?

29. **A** ○ I will pack my clothes toys and books.
    B ○ I will pack my clothes, toys, and books.
    C ○ I will pack, my clothes, toys, and, books.

Read the paragraph. Answer the questions.

Saturday is the best day of the week for me. I can sleep later in the morning. I go shopping with my family. Sometimes I ride my bike to my friend's house.

1. Choose the sentence that gives the main idea.

A ○ Saturday is the best day of the week for me.

B ○ I can sleep later in the morning.

C ○ Sometimes I ride my bike to my friend's house.

2. Choose the sentence that gives a detail about the main idea.

A ○ Saturday is the best day of the week for me.

B ○ I can sleep later in the morning.

C ○ My brother likes Mondays.

Read the paragraph. Answer the questions.

Amy's old skates were too small. First, she saved all her birthday money. Next, she went shopping with her aunt. Then she bought new skates that fit.

3. Choose what happened first.

A ○ Amy bought new skates that fit.

B ○ Amy went shopping with her aunt.

C ○ Amy saved all her birthday money.

4. Choose what happened last.

A ○ Amy's old skates were too small.

B ○ Amy bought new skates that fit.

C ○ Amy saved all her birthday money.

Name _____

Look at the letter. Choose the correct name for each numbered part of the letter.

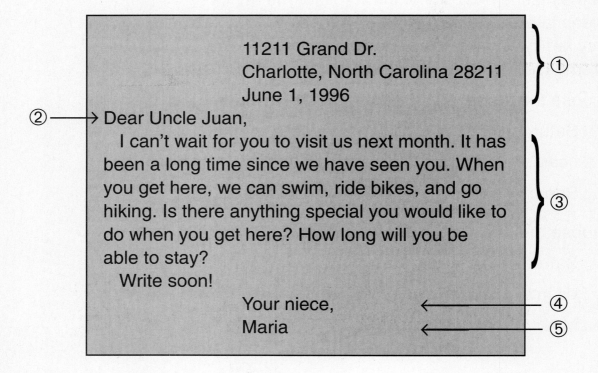

11211 Grand Dr.
Charlotte, North Carolina 28211
June 1, 1996 — ①

② → Dear Uncle Juan,

I can't wait for you to visit us next month. It has been a long time since we have seen you. When you get here, we can swim, ride bikes, and go hiking. Is there anything special you would like to do when you get here? How long will you be able to stay? — ③

Write soon!

Your niece, ← ④
Maria ← ⑤

5. What is part 1 of the letter called?

A ○ closing   B ○ heading   C ○ body

6. What is part 4 of the letter called?

A ○ heading   B ○ greeting   C ○ closing

7. What is part 5 of the letter called?

A ○ name   B ○ closing   C ○ greeting

8. What is part 3 of the letter called?

A ○ closing   B ○ heading   C ○ body

9. What is part 2 of the letter called?

A ○ body   B ○ greeting   C ○ name